The Mermaids and the Dolphin

Written by Celia Warren
Illustrated by Jessica Secheret

Bella and Anna lived in the sea.
They were playing with their pets.

“Look, there is Jo!” said Anna.
Jo was with
her pet crab Henry.
He was shy.

“Can Henry do tricks?”
said Anna.
“Our pets can!”

"Henry can hide his legs!"
said Jo.

“That is not very good,”
said Anna.

The mermaids heard a noise.
"What was that?" they asked.

They went to see.

The mermaids saw a dolphin.

"The dolphin is stuck in the net," said Bella. "He needs help!"

Henry helped the dolphin.
He cut the net
with his claws.

The dolphin was free!
"You are smart, Henry!"
said Anna.

"Thank you, Henry," said the dolphin.
He gave the mermaids some stars.

Bella and Anna put their stars in their hair.

Jo put her star on Henry!
"You **are** the star, Henry!"
she said.